The Psychology of Negotiation

Understanding the Key to Conflict Resolution

Naomi Ivy Francis

Table of Contents

1. Introduction 2
2. The Power of Negotiation: An Introduction 3
    2.1. The Essence of Negotiation 3
    2.2. The Impact of Effective Negotiation 3
    2.3. The Myriad Stages of Negotiation 4
    2.4. The Ethos of Negotiation 5
3. Decoding Negotiation: Understanding the Basics 6
    3.1. The Essence of Negotiation 6
    3.2. Types of Negotiation 7
4. The Human Factor: Psychology's Role in Negotiation 9
    4.1. Unveiling the Psychology of Negotiation 9
    4.2. The Central Role of Perception 10
    4.3. Riding the Wave of Emotion 10
    4.4. Harnessing Cognitive Processes 11
    4.5. The Power of Motivation 11
5. Emotional Intelligence: Unlocking Superior Negotiations 12
    5.1. The Essence of Emotional Intelligence 12
    5.2. Emotional Intelligence and Empathy in Negotiations 13
    5.3. Enhancing Interpersonal Skills Through Emotional Intelligence 13
    5.4. Cultivating Emotional Intelligence 14
6. Breaking Impasses: Strategies and Techniques 15
    6.1. Understanding the Impasse 15
    6.2. Maintaining open and flexible communication 15
    6.3. Enhancing Listening Skills 16
    6.4. Shifting the Frame 16
    6.5. Utilizing 'What-If' Scenarios 16
    6.6. Invoking a Higher Authority 17

- 6.7. Incorporating Rest Periods 17
- 6.8. Compromise and Concession Strategy 17
- 6.9. Deadlock Declaration 17
- 7. In Their Shoes: The Art and Science of Empathy in Negotiations . . . 19
  - 7.1. Awakening Emotional Responses 19
  - 7.2. The Dichotomy of Cognitive and Affective Empathy 19
  - 7.3. Empathy as a Steering Mechanism 20
  - 7.4. Empathy Mapping: A Visual Assembly of Perspectives 20
  - 7.5. Creating an Empathy Bridge 21
  - 7.6. The Pitfalls of Empathy and the Professional Distancing 21
- 8. Mastering Persuasion: The Role of Influence in Successful Negotiation 23
  - 8.1. Understanding the Power of Persuasion and Influence 23
  - 8.2. Principles of Persuasion 24
  - 8.3. Strategies to Hone Persuasive Influence in Negotiation 25
  - 8.4. Common Barriers to Successful Persuasion 26
- 9. Overcoming Barriers: Undressing Cognitive Biases in Negotiations 28
  - 9.1. The Nature of Cognitive Biases 28
  - 9.2. Navigating and Overcoming Anchoring Bias 29
  - 9.3. Quantifying and Addressing Confirmation Bias 29
  - 9.4. A Broader Perspective: Understanding Other Cognitive Biases 30
  - 9.5. Conclusion: The Journey towards Biases-Free Negotiation . . . 30
- 10. From Conflict to Resolution: Negotiating Difficult Situations . . . 32
  - 10.1. Unveiling the Concept of Conflict in Negotiation 32
  - 10.2. Embracing Conflict: First Steps towards Resolution 33
  - 10.3. Communicating Effectively: The Key to Resolving Conflict . . 33
  - 10.4. Deploying Conflict Resolution Strategies 34
  - 10.5. Moving From Conflict to Resolution: Conclusion 34

11. Road to Mastery: Building Effective and Sustainable
Negotiation Skills 36
    11.1. The Art of Continuous Learning 36
    11.2. Dancing with Adaptability 37
    11.3. Beyond Tactics: Embodying a Negotiator's Mindset 37
    11.4. Practice Makes Permanent 38

Negotiation in the classic diplomatic sense assumes parties more anxious to agree than to disagree.

— Dean Acheson

Chapter 1. Introduction

Introducing our Special Report "The Psychology of Negotiation: Understanding the Key to Conflict Resolution". In this fascinating journey into one of the most critical aspects of human interaction, we unveil the secrets of effective negotiation, providing a refreshing take on how to turn conflict into opportunity. This engaging report is far from a dull technical manual. Instead, it's an excitement-packed exploration of the human mind and behavior, filled with practical insights and real-world applications that have the power to elevate your negotiations, both professional and personal. Bursting with enlightening content, our Special Report is tailor-made just for you, designed to capture your intellect, stimulate your curiosity, and inspire you to act. Stake your claim on a world of untold possibilities at the negotiation table — pick up this Special Report today!

Chapter 2. The Power of Negotiation: An Introduction

A negotiation, in essence, is the dynamic process where different parties engage to reach mutually beneficial agreements. It is an indispensable tool, a power, wielded by diplomats and businesspeople alike, employed in boardrooms and private conversations, necessary in both broad-brushed political and finely-detailed familial contexts.

2.1. The Essence of Negotiation

Each negotiation begins with the understanding that stakeholders have divergent interests, but there is an underlying presumption of potential consensus. Negotiation is a dance between the desire for self-interest and the necessity for mutual gain. It is an adventure embarked upon by individuals or groups with the intention, belief, and faith that they can arrive at a satisfying conclusion acceptable to all.

Negotiations are not limited to high-stakes business deals or diplomatic discussions. In reality, they are an integral part of our everyday lives. Whether it's haggling at a flea market, convincing a child to go to bed on time, or determining household chores among roommates, these are all negotiations at heart. The concept interweaves itself in professional and domestic settings, underlining the importance of understanding its facets.

2.2. The Impact of Effective Negotiation

The power and impact of effective negotiation are immense. A successful negotiation brings about win-win situations—the holy grail of negotiation outcomes. Both parties walk away feeling like victors, thereby strengthening the relationship and setting the stage for future positive interactions. It's not just about gaining or conceding; effective negotiation genuinely seeks to enhance the situation for all involved.

Simply put, negotiation expertise lends you the power to influence outcomes in your favor, leading to personal or professional growth. It provides you with a distinct edge, an essential bargaining tool in the chaotic and fast-paced world we reside in today.

2.3. The Myriad Stages of Negotiation

Think of negotiation as a journey. It unfolds over various stages, each with its own unique dynamics, challenges, strategies, and results. One starts by preparing, defining, and understanding one's objectives and stakes. Knowing what you want—and, crucially, what you are willing to give—is fundamental to embarking on a negotiation.

Following the preparation, the negotiation proper commences. Here, dialogue, interaction, persuasion, compromise, and hard bargaining all come into play. Different tactics and strategies are employed at different stages, as the negotiation waxes and wanes, responding to the changing circumstances and information landscapes.

The process concludes with either a successful agreement or an impasse. In both situations, pragmatic learnings can be extrapolated, making every negotiation an opportunity for growth. So, even in 'failure', the power of negotiation persists, offering lessons for handling similar future challenges.

2.4. The Ethos of Negotiation

Inherent to the idea of negotiation is a certain ethos. Foremost, a respect for the process is required, recognizing its potential to reach accord where there would be discord otherwise. Secondly, a respect for the other party also maintains the integrity of the process. Bullying tactics might win the day, but they poison the well for future interactions. So, the principle of 'fair play' underpins truly effective negotiation.

Additionally, negotiation is not a one-size-fits-all process. Each circumstance demands its own cocktail of approaches, requiring negotiators to be flexible, adaptable, and innovative.

Understanding and harnessing the power of negotiation can undoubtedly be an empowering tool in the grand theatre of life, bearing impact at a micro (personal) and macro (organizational and societal) level. In our pursuit of mastering this skill, the ensuing chapters will journey through what makes negotiation tick. From grasping the basic principles, delving into the psychological aspects, understanding emotional intelligence, breaking impasses, empathy, persuasion, overcoming barriers, negotiating tough situations and finally, to building effective negotiation skills, we will comprehensively explore how to wield the power of negotiation effectively.

Chapter 3. Decoding Negotiation: Understanding the Basics

Negotiation, despite being ubiquitous, is often misunderstood by many. Some perceive it as a battle of wits, others as a chance to aggressively bargain, while many see it as an anxious confrontation. Shedding light on the true essence of this complex human behavior requires an attentive dive into its foundational elements, a keen exploration of its nature, its core principles as well as distilling certain misconceptions that often surround it.

The intent of this chapter is to decipher negotiation, illuminate its aspects, and lay a strong foundation for the chapters that follow. We'll delve into the complexities of negotiation, taking special care to ensure the content is designed to foster understanding and provoke curiosity rather than confound. We'll be patient explorers of this domain, weaving through the tangled labyrinth of concepts with a steady stride and a clear vision.

3.1. The Essence of Negotiation

Any social interaction involving decision-making can be seen as a negotiation. Two or more parties, each with their own sets of interests and perspective, come together to reach a mutually beneficial outcome. It's important to understand that a negotiation extends beyond the traditional bargaining over a price or haggling at a market place. The realm expands from international diplomacy, corporate acquisitions, legal settlements to everyday situations like deciding on a family vacation or resolving a dispute among coworkers. Fundamentally, negotiation is a process-oriented, reciprocal endeavor that seeks to reach agreement.

The building blocks of negotiation are 'value', 'relationship', and 'power'. These three elements dance around each other in a delicate ballet that forms a successful negotiation process. Value is all about what is at stake and what can be gained or lost. Relationships are crucial to understand the mutual interdependence among parties and how it influences the negotiation. Power, on the other hand, is an elusive element that can greatly influence the outcomes based on how it is used or perceived.

Next, we look at these components separately to understand them in greater depth:

1. Value: The core element for both parties involved in the negotiation. Understanding what each party values, allows for the creation of a common ground, a basis for 'give and take', while expanding the opportunity for mutual gains.
2. Relationship: Understanding the dynamics, the history, and the nature of the relationship between the parties plays a significant role in how the negotiation unfolds. Relationships can influence attitudes, behaviors, and the overall course of the negotiation.
3. Power: This is about perceived leverage, the influence one party can exercise over the other. It's about authority, resources, and knowledge. Power dynamics could shift during the process as influencing factors change.

3.2. Types of Negotiation

Negotiations can be broadly classified into two types: distributive and integrative.

In a Distributive negotiation, also known as zero-sum or win-lose negotiation, the mentality is that one party's gain is another's loss. Imagine slicing a pie; the larger somebody's slice, the smaller the remaining pie for the rest. These negotiations are often about a singular issue, typically price. They're considerably competitive and the relationship between parties might not take center stage.

On the other hand, Integrative negotiations, or win-win negotiations, revolve around the conviction that mutual gains are possible. The parties believe that the pie can be expanded rather than sliced. They encourage collaboration and creativity to uncover commonalities and reconcile differences. They focus on multiple issues, allowing trade-offs and concessions for reaching beneficial agreements. The relationship aspect is given importance considering the potential for future engagements.

Each type of negotiation requires varying approaches, tactics, and mindsets. Pinpointing the nature of the negotiation at hand provides the initial cue on how to proceed, what to expect, and how to prepare.

By the end of this enlightening chapter, we hope you've developed a deeper understanding of negotiation and its foundations, preparing you to take on the world of negotiation with a renewed eagerness. As we proceed further, we will continue to build upon these basics, with successive chapters diving into more detailed aspects of negotiation psychology, influence, and tactics.

Chapter 4. The Human Factor: Psychology's Role in Negotiation

The intersection of psychology and negotiation forms not merely a crossroad, but a broad, intricate highway overpass where multiple lanes of human understanding convene. It's on this complex structure where we delve into the human mind's role in determining the course and outcome of negotiation processes. Simply put, when we invite psychology to the negotiation table, it sheds light on various aspects of human behavior. Through applying psychological lenses, we aim to better understand how thoughts, feelings, emotions, and perceptions shape our negotiation styles and strategies, as well as how these elements can be channeled to achieve optimal outcomes.

4.1. Unveiling the Psychology of Negotiation

Far from being a simple transactional process, negotiation is heavily influenced by the human mind's intricacies, displaying our motives, apprehensions, aspirations, and hesitations. From cognitive biases that color our understanding to the emotional undercurrents that sway our decisions, the landscape of negotiation is sculpted by a rich tapestry of psychological variables.

The psychological perspective of negotiation invites us to appreciate this process, not just as a method to reach agreements, but as a labyrinth of human emotions, cognitions, and interpersonal dynamics. By peeling the complex layers of negotiation through the lens of psychology, we unveil the subtle and not-so-subtle forces that shape the essence of our negotiation journeys.

4.2. The Central Role of Perception

Perception forms the underlying tapestry upon which all negotiation interactions are painted. How we perceive others' intentions, motivations, needs, fears, and the nature of the negotiation setting can significantly influence how we interact and respond. As each party enters the negotiation arena, they do so with a set of preconceived perceptions shaped by past experiences, beliefs, and individual worldviews. Understanding these perceptual patterns is crucial in steering the negotiation process towards mutual gain and collaboration.

In turn, the other party's perception of us also significantly influences the negotiation trajectory. Striving to manage their perception and concurrently staying open to challenge and change our perceptions is a critical balancing act in negotiation.

4.3. Riding the Wave of Emotion

Emotions, like the mighty oceans, are powerful, deep, and often unpredictable. They permeate the negotiation process, influencing thought processes, guiding reactions, and shaping negotiation outcomes. Understanding and effectively managing our own emotions and those of others in a negotiation setting can tilt the scales towards a more effective and satisfactory deal for all parties involved.

Valuable emotional skills in negotiation include emotional self-awareness, which refers to recognizing our own emotional states; emotional management, which entails regulating our emotions to respond rather than react during negotiation; and empathy, which involves understanding and appreciating the emotional reality of the other party.

4.4. Harnessing Cognitive Processes

To a considerable extent, cognition pilots negotiation outcomes. From setting initial negotiation goals to formulating strategies, making decisions, assessing risks, and finally, deciding on the acceptability of the proposed agreement, cognitive processes underscore every stage of a negotiation. Awareness of these cognitive patterns can offer strategically advantageous negotiation insights.

Common cognitive concerns in negotiation include framing, which is how we perceive and present information; cognitive biases, which are systematic but subconscious errors in thinking that can impair decision making; and heuristics, which are mental shortcuts that we use when making decisions, particularly under conditions of uncertainty or information overload.

4.5. The Power of Motivation

Motivation influences negotiation in substantial ways, impacting our drive, intentionality, and level of engagement. It also shapes whether we approach the negotiation competitively, seeking personal gain, or cooperatively, looking for a mutually beneficial solution. A strong understanding of the motivational forces at play can lead us to more strategic and effective negotiation approaches.

In conclusion, psychology plays an integral part in negotiation. By understanding and applying key psychological principles, we can engage in more effective and strategic negotiation, turning potential conflict into opportunity. Whether through managing perceptions, emotional states, cognitive processes, or motivations, leveraging psychology can empower us to navigate the negotiation landscape more proficiently and productively.

Chapter 5. Emotional Intelligence: Unlocking Superior Negotiations

In the labyrinthine complexity of negotiations, emotional intelligence leverages a powerful advantage, letting you navigate the process with a superior understanding of human emotions and interpersonal dynamics. This chapter delves deep into the compelling role of emotional intelligence in orchestrating successful negotiations.

5.1. The Essence of Emotional Intelligence

The cornerstone of emotional intelligence is self-awareness, the capacity to comprehend one's emotions and their effects. A high degree of self-awareness helps individuals recognize their emotional triggers, comprehend their strengths and weaknesses, and develop the capability to manage themselves effectively. This understanding is particularly critical during negotiations, where feelings of anxiety, frustration, or excitement can significantly impact the outcome.

Imbued with self-awareness, an emotionally intelligent negotiator can regulate their emotions competently. They attune themselves to their internal emotional landscapes, rehearsing responses to potential triggers and skillfully calibrating their reactions. This emotional regulation serves as a bulwark, protecting from impulsive or overly charged emotional outbursts that could derail negotiations.

Self-awareness begets another vital component of emotional intelligence- self-motivation. It is what drives individuals to persist in the face of setbacks, and channel their emotional energy towards the negotiation goal. During tenacious negotiations, an individual's self-motivation can spell the difference between capitulation and fruitful resolution.

5.2. Emotional Intelligence and Empathy in Negotiations

Equally, an emotionally intelligent negotiator wields empathy as a potent tool. By tuning into the emotional wavelength of their counterparts, they demonstrate an understanding of others' feelings, concerns, and perspectives. Such reciprocity can defuse tension, foster trust, and facilitate amicable resolution.

Exhibiting empathy, however, does not equate to ceding ground in negotiations. On the contrary, it offers invaluable insights into the other party's motivations and goals, allowing strategies to be tailored for optimal results. An empathetic negotiator can align their proposals with their counterpart's interests, making acceptance more likely.

Moreover, an empathetic approach can shed light on non-verbal cues and underlying sentiments, which often speak louder than words. Awareness of these subtleties provides an additional layer of information, enhancing the ability to respond appropriately and effectively.

5.3. Enhancing Interpersonal Skills Through Emotional Intelligence

Finally, emotional intelligence bolsters interpersonal skills, an attribute indispensable in any negotiation. Interpersonal skills cement the bond between negotiators, fostering a climate of mutual respect and open communication. Emotionally intelligent individuals, adept at fostering positive interpersonal relationships, contribute towards a more cooperative negotiation environment.

They possess the knack of assertive communication, articulating their point without engendering hostility. They sagaciously manage conflicts by acknowledging differences and working towards common ground rather than letting disagreements escalate.

5.4. Cultivating Emotional Intelligence

Understanding the role of emotional intelligence in negotiations is just the beginning. Cultivating it demands introspection and practice. Begin by attuning to your emotions, acknowledging them without judgment. Also, strive to comprehend others' perspectives, fostering empathy. Practice active listening, pay attention to non-verbal cues, and work on refining your interpersonal skills. Remember, emotional intelligence, much like other skills, can be enhanced with deliberate practice and consistent efforts.

In conclusion, emotional intelligence unlocks a superior approach to negotiations. By understanding and managing emotions—both ours and others—we can tactfully navigate the complex interpersonal dynamic that shapes a negotiation. Embracing emotional intelligence empowers us to find mutual ground, thus propelling negotiations towards successful outcomes.

By intertwining emotional intelligence with negotiation strategies, this chapter has shed light on how emotions, when managed deftly, can shift from being potential obstacles to powerful aids in negotiation. As we delve further into aspects of negotiation in the subsequent chapters, this understanding will prove to be an invaluable resource.

Chapter 6. Breaking Impasses: Strategies and Techniques

Impasses, or stalemates as some may know them, are a common occurrence in negotiations and can serve as significant hurdles to reaching successful agreements. However, they should not be viewed as insurmountable obstacles. Instead, imagine them as intricate puzzles with multiple pieces (read: strategies and techniques) that can be assembled to find a solution.

6.1. Understanding the Impasse

An impasse happens when negotiation parties reach a point where they cannot move forward due to differing or opposing views. It may occur due to an array of reasons like conflicting interests, power imbalance, or even emotional hurdles. It can lead to negotiations getting trapped in a destructive loop, stifling progress.

This is where impasse-breaking strategies come into play. The negotiation table is not just a place for discussions – it is a conduit for persuasion, creativity, and tact. Let's delve into the vast array of strategies available to us.

6.2. Maintaining open and flexible communication

A major cause of impasse during negotiations is poor or rigid communication. Open, non-judgemental communication lays the foundation for creative problem solving. It often entails risk-taking, as both parties may have to share information they initially deemed confidential. Mutual trust and respect during this process facilitate an atmosphere conducive to problem-solving and, eventually, breaking the impasse.

6.3. Enhancing Listening Skills

While actively presenting one's viewpoint is essential, an oft-neglected aspect of negotiation is being an effective listener. Engaging empathetic listening allows for a deeper understanding of the opposing party's perspective. This understanding often opens avenues for creative solutions, which may otherwise stay hidden. Active listening involves responding and asking questions, confirming the feeling and facts, and summarizing to ensure understanding.

6.4. Shifting the Frame

Perception holds a relentless grip on reality. Therefore, reframing the issue or shifting the frame can help view the problem from a different vantage point. Shifting away from a win-lose scenario to a win-win situation may require exploring shared interests or long-term mutual benefits, pushing the negotiation towards a collaborative problem-solving approach.

6.5. Utilizing 'What-If' Scenarios

A potential approach to breaking an impasse is by playing out 'what-if' scenarios. This technique couples creativity with foresight. It allows parties to explore various possible outcomes and the potential ramifications of each option, adding a fresh perspective to the negotiation, which may lead to creative solutions and compromises.

6.6. Invoking a Higher Authority

A third-party authority with higher power (a boss, a parent organization, or a board of directors) can often help resolve a stalemate. This intervention can provide new inputs, mediate the process, or even impose a decision. This strategy should be used judiciously to ensure it doesn't underplay the legitimacy of the negotiation or aggrieve any party involved.

6.7. Incorporating Rest Periods

Contrary to common beliefs, negotiations are intrinsically exhaustive. Both mental and emotional factors heavily laden the process and are potential impasse-triggerers. Incorporating rest periods during the process allows parties to recharge, reflect, and potentially reassess their positions. This can lead to the surfacing of new insights and strategies to handle the impasse.

6.8. Compromise and Concession Strategy

While negotiation often involves protecting one's interests, arriving at a mutually acceptable compromise can break an impasse. Concessions should be considered carefully, ensuring at the very least your minimum acceptable gains. Making a concession could reinstate faith in the process, pushing parties out of the deadlock.

6.9. Deadlock Declaration

On the surface, declaring a deadlock may seem counter-intuitive. However, it carries a strategic value. It may nudge parties out of their trenches, prompting them to either reconsider previously rejected proposals or present new concessions. It signals the risk of negotiation failure, possibly igniting urgency.

These impasse-breaking strategies are akin to a rich toolset. Each negotiation is unique, creating a need for different tools or combinations at different times. Keen understanding and effective deployment of these strategies can pave the way for a negotiation victory, turning your impasses into pathways and setting up a stage for meaningful, successful dialogues, ultimately leading to the actualization of win-win scenarios. While the impasse may initially signify a discord, the effective use of these strategies can orchestrate harmony out of cacophony, leading to the resolution of conflicts in the most profound manner.

Chapter 7. In Their Shoes: The Art and Science of Empathy in Negotiations

To understand and master the art and science of empathy in negotiations, one must first embrace the complexity and richness of this concept, laying the groundwork for an expansive and exhaustive journey. Empathy, at its very core, is the capacity to understand or feel what another person is experiencing from within their frame of reference – that is, to place oneself in another's shoes.

7.1. Awakening Emotional Responses

Emotional responses are entwined with the foundations of empathy. When someone expresses strong emotions, acknowledging them can diffuse potential tension and facilitate effective communication. Recognizing the emotions at play isn't confined to the other party; it is essential to be aware of and manage your own feelings in the negotiation. Emotional self-recognition primes us for a better understanding of others, laying a potent groundwork for emulative empathy.

7.2. The Dichotomy of Cognitive and Affective Empathy

Two key types of empathy are fundamental to negotiation - cognitive and affective. Cognitive empathy refers to our ability to understand someone else's perspective or mental state, while affective empathy deals with sharing their emotions. It's this intricate interplay of thought and feeling that posits empathy as a pivotal force in successful negotiations.

In cognitive empathy, we intentionally try to understand a situation from the other's viewpoint. It involves the conscious effort to put aside our biases and preconceived notions to truly 'see' the situation from another's perspective. On the other hand, affective empathy engages our emotional faculties. We feel what the other person feels, sharing in their joy, disappointment, anxiety, or excitement. However, it's critical to keep such shared feelings in check to avoid being swept away by the emotional undercurrents, which could detrimentally influence the negotiation process.

7.3. Empathy as a Steering Mechanism

Skilful negotiators adeptly use empathy as a steering mechanism in their interactions. It paves the way for trust, encourages open communication, and supports collaborative problem-solving. Empathy helps to frame the negotiation narrative positively, laying the groundwork for robust, future-proof agreements steeped in mutual respect and understanding. It enables negotiators to connect with people, highlighting shared objectives and common ground, while respecting differences and divergent interests.

7.4. Empathy Mapping: A Visual Assembly of Perspectives

Empathy mapping offers a concrete tool for negotiators to grasp their counterparts' perspectives systematically. An empathy map is a simple, visual tool designed to articulate what we know about a particular user. It externalizes knowledge about users in order to create a shared understanding of user needs during the negotiation process. The four quadrants of an empathy map typically represent

'Says,' 'Thinks,' 'Does,' and 'Feels,' capturing a holistic perspective of the other party's standpoint.

7.5. Creating an Empathy Bridge

Building an empathy bridge involves the creation of a two-way understanding that connects negotiators at a deeper level. It involves sharing personal feelings, perceptions, and motivations to help each other gain insight into their respective positions. By choosing appropriate words, employing active listening, making concerted efforts to understand each other's emotions, and expressing them, negotiators can foster an environment that promotes shared understanding and stronger negotiation outcomes.

7.6. The Pitfalls of Empathy and the Professional Distancing

While empathy is valuable in negotiations, it's important to understand its limitations. It can lead to potential biases, emotional contagion, and loss of objectivity. Professional distancing involves setting appropriate emotional boundaries, so empathy aids the negotiation process without undermining it. Striking this delicate balance allows negotiators to connect emotionally while maintaining the pragmatic detachment necessary for objective decision-making.

Cultivating and applying empathy in negotiations paves the way for an enhanced, more profound understanding of the universality of human experience. A wealth of possibilities opens up in the realm of negotiation when we step out of our shoes and step into the shoes of those with whom we negotiate. This intricate dance of emotional intelligence paints the picture for a new brand of negotiations, one that inspires respect, mutual understanding, and the creation of value for all parties involved. By painting this colourful canvas of shared human experience, we can turn the task of negotiation into an art.

Chapter 8. Mastering Persuasion: The Role of Influence in Successful Negotiation

Diving headfirst into the labyrinth intricacies of negotiation, persuasion is a pivotal element of the process, serving as the linchpin between success and failure in many situations. The role of influence in successful negotiation cannot be understated, manifesting as a subtle but powerful factor that can tilt the balance in one's favor during discussions. Fittingly, it expands far beyond just "making others see your perspective". Influence encompasses constructing favorable circumstances, sculpting the discourse, and deliberately shaping the negotiation environment.

8.1. Understanding the Power of Persuasion and Influence

Persuasion is an art that deals with the deliberate effort to change, reshape, or impact someone's beliefs, attitudes, intentions, motivations, or behaviors. However, it is also a science that requires profound understanding, rigorous practice, and adept application. Effective persuasion is a cocktail of different psychological concepts, exercises in empathy, and an adept understanding of one's counterpart. While the ability to persuade does not guarantee a win in every negotiation scenario, it definitely increases one's chances manifold by fostering a conducive environment for collaboration and agreement.

In the realm of negotiation, influence involves shaping the decision-making process of the other negotiating party to meet your interests.

Negotiators who understand how to exert their influence can shape the negotiation's outcomes more effectively. But influence doesn't mean manipulation; rather, it's about understanding the balance of power dynamics in the discussion and leveraging that understanding to steer conversation constructively.

8.2. Principles of Persuasion

Dr. Robert Cialdini, a psychology and marketing professor, formulated six key principles of persuasian, which can readily apply to the context of negotiation. Numbered sequentially, the principles are: Reciprocity, Commitment and Consistency, Social Proof, Authority, Liking, and Scarcity.

1. **Reciprocity:** People are inherently wired to return a favor when they receive one. Accordingly, negotiators can utilize this principle by offering something valuable in the initial stages of the negotiation process. This instills a sense of obligation that can, in turn, positively influence the outcome.

2. **Commitment and Consistency:** Once a person takes a position or makes a promise, they are more likely to stick to it, even if it's not in their best interest. In negotiations, getting initial minor agreements can lead to larger commitments later.

3. **Social Proof:** This principle hinges on the concept that people will follow the actions of the mass. If negotiators can show that their proposals are accepted and supported by others, it may lead the other party to think and act likewise.

4. **Authority:** People are more likely to follow those they perceive as credible experts. Hence, negotiators who can convincingly demonstrate their expertise or authority in a certain area are more likely to persuade the other party to their viewpoint.

5. **Liking:** We are naturally more prone to agree with people we like or find similar to ourselves. Therefore, building rapport at the beginning of negotiations might swing the balance in your favor.

6. **Scarcity:** The principle of scarcity indicates that people place higher value on things that seem scarce or exclusive. In the context of negotiation, emphasizing the uniqueness or limited availability of your offer can increase its perceived value.

8.3. Strategies to Hone Persuasive Influence in Negotiation

Negotiation is often akin to a pooling game of interests where influence may shift rapidly among the involved parties. To hone persuasive influence, one needs to adhere to specific strategies that have been tested through time and reaffirmed by practical experiences.

Preparation and Understanding: Start by gaining a thorough understanding of the other party's needs, motivations, and constraints, which can serve as an effective persuasion tool. This information serves as the linchpin of your negotiation strategy, enabling you to align your arguments and responses. After all, it is far easier to persuade someone when you are speaking their language and addressing their concerns.

Building Trust and Credibility: Trust and credibility are the cornerstones of any negotiation, serving as the foundation upon which successful influence is built. People are more likely to be persuaded by those they trust and respect. Therefore, demonstrate your competence and reliability early on, and be consistent in your actions and words.

Rhetorical Strategies: Master the subtleties of verbal and nonverbal communication. The way an argument is framed can drastically influence how it's received. For instance, people generally avoid risks when a particular option is presented in a positive, gain-framed messaging but might take risks when the same option is framed negatively, or as a loss.

Emotional Intelligence: This ability to understand and manage emotions significantly affects the negotiation process. Being aware of your own emotional state and being sensitive to others' emotions can help you navigate the negotiation process more smoothly.

8.4. Common Barriers to Successful Persuasion

Despite its great potential, persuasion can encounter barriers. Understanding these obstacles can equip negotiators with extra tools in turning conversations in their favor.

Resistance to Change: People are usually inclined towards maintaining the status quo, making it difficult to convince them to adopt a new perspective or approach.

Different Belief Systems: Contrasting belief systems can impede persuasion as individuals might hold on to their perceptions tightly, making it hard to see the situation from your viewpoint.

Mistrust: A lack of trust will render even the most potent of persuasive efforts ineffective. It's therefore critical to establish trust early in the process.

Skepticism: Invariably, negotiators might enter conversations with a degree of skepticism, expecting attempts to manipulate or exploit them. Exhibiting transparency and authenticity can help alleviate these fears.

By understanding the concept, principles, strategies, and barriers of persuasion, negotiators can use influence as a powerful tool in the negotiation arena. In conclusion, underpinning the art of persuasion lies the core emphasis on empathy, understanding, and mutual benefit. While influence provides the ability to mold situations in a favorable manner, it should not descend into manipulation, but evolve as a factor in creating value and forging ties based on trust, respect, and collaborative achievement.

Chapter 9. Overcoming Barriers: Undressing Cognitive Biases in Negotiations

In our exploration into the complex yet fascinating realm of negotiations, it is crucial to consider the role of cognitive biases and the impact they have on the negotiation process. These mental shortcuts, whilst useful in some contexts, can pose significant barriers to effective negotiation. Unaddressed, they can skew our perspective, distort our judgement, and consequently, impede objective decision-making.

9.1. The Nature of Cognitive Biases

Cognitive biases are systematic errors in our thinking that influence the judgements and decisions we make. They are not random errors, rather they are patterns of deviations from standard rationality. These biases occur due to our brains' attempt to simplify information processing. At times, these simplifications prove efficient and useful, while at others, they distort our perception of reality. Cognitive biases come in many forms and can significantly impact the negotiation process.

One of the most prominent examples of these biases in negotiation contexts is the anchoring bias, where early, initial information significantly influences the course of negotiation. For instance, the first price suggested in a negotiation can often 'anchor' the ensuing negotiations, steering the range and nature of counteroffers. Similarly, the confirmation bias leads us to favor information that confirms our existing beliefs, often leading us to overemphasize supporting data while overlooking contradictory information.

This chapter aims to illuminate such cognitive biases and provide you with strategies to navigate and overcome them, thereby enhancing your negotiation skills.

9.2. Navigating and Overcoming Anchoring Bias

An essential step to overcoming anchoring bias is being aware of its presence. As negotiators, we should come to the table well-equipped, having conducted diligent research and market analysis in advance to help us recognize and resist inappropriate anchors. It is essential that we be the one to take the initiative and make the first offer, thus potentially setting the anchor ourselves, after carefully weighing in all the relevant factors.

Additionally, understanding the psychological process behind the bias gives us the power to anticipate its influence and strategically adjust our responses. We can cultivate a habit of questioning all our judgements and decisions to ensure that they are free from any anchoring bias.

9.3. Quantifying and Addressing Confirmation Bias

Confirmation bias is a relentless cognitive skew. We continuously perceive the world through a filter of personal interpretations and judgments. It results in a lopsided information processing during negotiations, as we tend to undervalue opposing arguments and overvalue supporting information.

To overcome the confirmation bias, it is necessary to actively seek out contradictory information and perspectives. We need to diversify our sources of information, consider multiple viewpoints, and question our existing beliefs. Challenging our notions and judgments helps us make more balanced decisions, leading to more equitable negotiations.

Another strategy to combat confirmation bias is using techniques like the "pre-mortem" – imagining that the negotiation has failed, and then working backwards, analyzing the factors that may have contributed to this failure. This can help to broaden our understanding and consideration of potential pitfalls, thus helping to mitigate the bias.

9.4. A Broader Perspective: Understanding Other Cognitive Biases

While anchoring and confirmation biases are common and particularly impactful in negotiations, they are by no means exhaustive. It becomes crucial, therefore, to appreciate and understand other cognitive biases and their manifestations. This includes biases like the overconfidence bias, where negotiators overestimate their ability or the accuracy of their information, or the sunk-cost fallacy, where past investments (in terms of time, resources, or efforts) unduly influence future negotiation decisions.

By investing time in understanding these biases, you can preempt their potential influence and devise strategies to counteract them. This expansion of awareness is fundamental to improving your negotiation acumen, thus allowing you to engage and emerge successful in negotiation situations more effectively.

9.5. Conclusion: The Journey towards Biases-Free Negotiation

Understanding and overcoming cognitive biases isn't about attaining flawless cognition; it's about recognizing our cognitive pitfalls and developing strategies to mitigate their impact on our judgments and decisions. It's about fostering a mindset that's driven by evidence, reason, empathy, and humility - a mindset that appreciates the complexity and diversity of thought and perception that a negotiation table brings.

By adopting a bias-free lens, we promote a negotiation climate that's not just fair and objective, but also innovative and collaborative. Removing the distortions caused by cognitive biases can help us uncover novel solutions and foster the shared understanding needed for successful negotiation. It can transform conflictual negotiations to win-win outcomes, where parties don't just settle with the 'least bad' option, but actively create and explore possibilities that maximize mutual gains.

But remember, overcoming biases is an ongoing process. It involves continuous learning, reflections, and adjustments. It requires us to be humble, open, and patient, understanding that biases encapsulate years, often decades, of belief systems and experiences. As we continue on this journey, we'll realize that addressing and mitigating cognitive biases isn't just a negotiation skill, it's a life skill - one that enables us to understand better, communicate effectively, and connect deeply.

Thus, in our journey through the labyrinthine world of negotiations, understanding and overcoming cognitive biases pave the way for successful and satisfying outcomes - ensuring that we negotiate not just with our minds, but also with our hearts.

Chapter 10. From Conflict to Resolution: Negotiating Difficult Situations

Establishing a comprehension of conflict resolution begins with untangling the messy webs of human misunderstanding and disagreement, shedding light on the contrasts and disparities that exist within any negotiation scenario. Navigating through adverse circumstances requires a significant application of cognitive, emotional, and intuitive faculties, all aimed at overturning a possible conflict and driving it towards resolution.

10.1. Unveiling the Concept of Conflict in Negotiation

Negotiation is often likened to a dance — an intricate, delicate interplay of moves and countermoves, offers and counteroffers. But what happens when this dance is intruded upon by discordant tunes of disagreement and conflict? It's important to note that conflict is not an adverse occurrence to avoid in negotiation, but rather a potential avenue that propels the process of bargaining towards change. However, it is only through understanding the nature and causes of conflicts in negotiation that we can turn contentious situations into opportunities for agreement.

Conflict most frequently emerges in negotiation scenarios due to divergence in interests, misunderstandings, or misperceptions of the negotiation scenario or the other party's intentions. Such incongruities can result from differences in viewpoints, values, or priorities, triggering the onset of contention.

Decoding conflict requires intricate knowledge and understanding of its various forms and manifestations. Conflict can either be substantive, revolving around the negotiation's real issues, or emotional, rooted in distrust, frustration, or perceived disrespect, which can further complicate the path towards agreement.

10.2. Embracing Conflict: First Steps towards Resolution

To effectively address conflict and move towards resolution, it's essential to acknowledge the conflict's existence. This is an explicit recognition that negotiators need to approach with a positive frame of mind. Rolling up your sleeves and getting into the 'battle' can be fruitfully productive if the fight is understood to be for the collective benefit of arriving at a win-win situation.

On recognizing a conflict, practice active listening. Hear out the other party with the intent to understand rather than react. Skilful and empathic listening can help decipher the root causes of the conflict and provide crucial insights that can be instrumental in paving the way towards resolution.

10.3. Communicating Effectively: The Key to Resolving Conflict

Effective communication stands as an indispensable tool in transforming conflict into resolution. This involves expressing oneself clearly and without ambiguity, empathetically understanding the other party's viewpoint, and facilitating open and constructive dialogue.

A critical aspect of productive communication is the use of non-defensive language. By refraining from language aimed at attacking or criticizing the other party, negotiators can prevent the escalation of conflict and maintain a conducive environment for resolution.

Moreover, using 'I' statements can help express your viewpoint in a non-threatening manner, fostering a more open and receptive dialogue.

Another essential communication strategy is to formulate and ask open-ended questions. This encourages a more in-depth exploration of interests and concerns and may lead to important discoveries about the underlying issues fuelling the conflict.

10.4. Deploying Conflict Resolution Strategies

Once a sound understanding of the conflict is developed, effective conflict resolution strategies can be harnessed. Some of the popular strategies involve collaboration, where both parties cooperate to achieve a mutually beneficial solution. The strategy of accommodation involves one party conceding some points to preserve the relationship. Compromise, as the term suggests, involves both parties making some sacrifices for a middle-ground solution.

Still, the strategy chosen should reflect the overarching priorities of the negotiation - whether they are the deal's substance, the relationship, or a mix of both. Deploying appropriate strategies can help mitigate conflict and facilitate a conducive pathway to resolution.

10.5. Moving From Conflict to Resolution: Conclusion

Ultimately, transitioning from conflict to resolution in negotiation is not a linear, one-size-fits-all process. It involves a complex interplay of skills centered around understanding, communication, empathy, and strategic decision-making. It's a gradual process where understanding the conflict's nature paves the way for effective communication, which then enables the application of resolution strategies.

As the impasse unravels into understanding, a constructive conflict metamorphoses into a beacon of possibility, an opportunity to strike a deal that serves mutual interests and reinforces relationships. Let the dance continue, let the negotiation transcend, from conflict to resolution. Mastery of negotiating difficult situations does not imply an elimination of conflict but guiding it towards a harmonious resolution. Understanding and traversing this route is the very essence of effective negotiation.

Negotiation is a craft, a delicate art that balances human understanding, logical reasoning, and emotional intelligence. By understanding and employing these skills effectively, one can transform the rough ends of conflict into the smooth narrative of resolution, successfully navigating difficult situations towards favorable outcomes.

Chapter 11. Road to Mastery: Building Effective and Sustainable Negotiation Skills

Recognizing that negotiation is a critical skill to master in all life's spheres, the journey often begins with understanding the fundamentals of negotiation to developing mastery over intricate and delicate tactics. This ruminative path subsequently paves the way to a point where a negotiator becomes a maestro, commanding negotiations not only efficiently but also sustainably.

11.1. The Art of Continuous Learning

Foremost, the mastery of any skill, including negotiation, is a commitment to life-long learning. Even the most successful negotiators realize that one negotiation, no matter how carefully planned and executed, won't entirely mirror the next. The dynamics surrounding negotiations constantly evolve, featuring different players, varied interests, and alternating situations. Hence, the road to mastery is no straight line. It's a winding pathway punctuated with persistent learning, unlearning, and relearning.

The most adept negotiators embrace this notion by constantly surveying the negotiation landscape, gauging shifts and transformations, adapting their approaches accordingly. They prioritize acquiring new knowledge and skills while simultaneously honing existing ones. In reality, the journey of learning is unceasing, brimming with myriad opportunities and experiences which, approached with an open mind, provide the impetus to become superior negotiators.

11.2. Dancing with Adaptability

The second attribute of skilled negotiators on the path to mastery is their potent ability to adapt. This knack to be agile, to seamlessly alternate between negotiation styles, and to adjust strategies based on situational requirements is one that one can only obtain through experience and purposeful reflection.

Over time, these negotiators develop an uncanny ability to read different situations, and more importantly, the people involved in these situations. This level of understanding equips them with the capability to behave in a manner that is most likely to achieve the desired outcome. This 'adaptability quotient' is a formidable asset in a world where negotiation situations are becoming increasingly complex and unpredictable.

11.3. Beyond Tactics: Embodying a Negotiator's Mindset

While tactics and strategies are pivotal to successful negotiations, the mastery journey transcends beyond these technical aspects. It also includes cultivating a negotiator's mindset - a deeper sense of self-awareness, astute emotional intelligence, acute sensitivity to cognitive biases, and an empathetic understanding of the other party's perspectives.

This mental and emotional fortitude allows negotiators to minimize fallacies that could potentially weaken their negotiation position. Moreover, it empowers them to anticipate and counteract the tactics of their negotiation counterpart effectively. Cultivating this mindset is a lifelong journey involving constant introspection, self-assessment, and growth.

11.4. Practice Makes Permanent

Lastly, and possibly most critically, it is persistent practice that facilitates mastery over negotiation skills. It's fruitful to learn continuously, adapt strategically, and foster a negotiator's mindset. However, these qualities risk becoming dormancies if they are not put into action regularly.

Repetition engrains these skills, allowing them to flow seamlessly. The more a negotiator uses these skills, the more instinctive they become, thus, forming an integral part of their negotiating persona.

Negotiation is a springboard for growth, whether personal, professional, or institutional. Its mastery are treasures on this growth trajectory, thus making the road to mastery a key or cardinal journey. The constant learning and practice, the perpetual state of self-awareness and adaptability; these attributes concurrently are the sustaining force that strengthen a negotiator's path to mastery.

In essence, the road to mastery is not an endpoint, but a journey. It's about striving relentlessly for improvement, adapting assertively to change, and practicing rigorously the act of negotiation. The exciting adventure of negotiation mastery awaits. Embrace it with gusto and passion, for it is not just a road, but a pathway to unmeasurable success.

www.ingramcontent.com/pod-product-compliance
Lightning Source LLC
Chambersburg PA
CBHW070953220526
45471CB00007B/3018